Celebrating YOU and ME

Many Ways to
DRESS

Christy Peterson

Lerner Publications ◆ Minneapolis

On Sesame Street, we celebrate everyone!

In this series, readers will explore the different ways we eat, dress, play, and more. Recognizing our similarities and differences will teach little ones to be proud of themselves and appreciate the world around them. Together, we can all be smarter, stronger, and kinder.

Sincerely, the Editors at Sesame Workshop

Table of Contents

Choosing Clothes

We wear clothes every day. We choose different clothes for different reasons.

I wear my tutu
when I dance.

All Kinds of Clothing

If we are going outside, we dress for the weather. You might wear a coat if it's cold or a sun hat if it's sunny!

I wear my
rain boots
when it's wet
outside.

People who play
on a sports team
wear uniforms.
Their uniforms
match.

That way the players can tell who's on their team.

Sometimes our clothes tell others about our cultures and our traditions.

On Mexican Independence Day, my family wears traditional clothes. We dance and watch fireworks.

The hanbok is worn to festivals and celebrations.

My family is from Korea, and I wore a hanbok to celebrate my first birthday.

Sometimes people wear certain clothes because of their religion. These head coverings are called a patka and a turban.

These head coverings are called kippahs.

Some people always wear their kippah. Some wear their kippah only during prayer.

These women are wearing head coverings called hijabs. They also wear long dresses called abayas. Hijabs and abayas come in many colors.

I love learning about all kinds of clothes.

It doesn't matter what clothes you wear each day. Each day is a chance to be a friend.

I love being Julia's friend.

Proud to Be Me!

Grab a sheet of paper and something to draw with, like crayons or colored pencils. Draw yourself wearing your favorite outfit.

I love all the
patches I wear on
my vest.

Glossary

culture: the beliefs and way of life shared by a group of people

patka: a head covering that is typically worn before a turban. Patkas are often tied into a knot.

religion: a system of beliefs and traditions

uniform: clothing worn to perform a specific job or matching clothing worn by a group

weather: what conditions are like outside, including temperature and wind

Learn More

Bullard, Lisa. *Dress-Up Day: All Kinds of Clothes.* Minneapolis: Lerner Publications, 2022.

Cohan, Medeia. *Hats of Faith.* San Francisco: Chronicle Books, 2018.

Markovics, Pearl. *My Favorite Clothes.* New York: Bearport, 2019.

Index

Photo Acknowledgments

Image credits: BearFotos/Shutterstock.com, p. 4 (top); Anatoliy Karlyuk/Shutterstock.com, p. 4 (bottom left); Westend61/Getty Images, p. 4 (bottom right); LWA/Dann Tardif/Getty Images, p. 6 (left); Denis Kuvaev/Shutterstock.com, p. 6 (right); FatCamera/Getty Images, pp. 8-9; David Grossman/Alamy Stock Photo, p. 10; CraigRJD/Getty Images, p. 12; IndiaPix/IndiaPicture/Getty Images, p. 14; Sergio Mendoza Hochmann/Getty Images, p. 15; oneinchpunch/Shutterstock.com, p. 16; Ridofranz/Getty Images, p. 17; Ariel Skelley/DigitalVision/Getty Images, pp. 18-19; Inna Kirkorova/Shutterstock.com, p. 20.

Cover: David Grossman/Alamy Stock Photo; FatCamera/E+/Getty Images; Yobro10/Getty Images.

Lerner Publications Company
An imprint of Lerner Publishing Group, Inc.
241 First Avenue North
Minneapolis, MN 55401 USA

For reading levels and more information, look up this title at www.lernerbooks.com.

Main body text set in Mikado. Typeface provided by HVD.

Designer: Laura Otto Rinne

Library of Congress Cataloging-in-Publication Data

Names: Peterson, Christy, author.
Title: Many ways to dress / Christy Peterson.
Description: Minneapolis : Lerner Publications, 2023. | Series: Sesame Street celebrating you and me | Includes bibliographical references and index. | Audience: Ages 4-8 (provided by Lerner Publications) | Audience: Grades K-1 (provided by Lerner Publications) | Description based on print version record and CIP data provided by publisher; resource not viewed.
Identifiers: LCCN 2021050999 (print) | LCCN 2021051000 (ebook) | ISBN 9781728456201 (library binding) | ISBN 9781728463759 (paperback) | ISBN 9781728462073 (ebook)
Subjects: LCSH: Clothing and dress—Juvenile literature.
Classification: LCC GT518 (ebook) | LCC GT518 .P47 2022 (print) | DDC 391 23/eng/20211—dc30

LC record available at https://lccn.loc.gov/2021050999
LC record available at https://lccn.loc.gov/2021051000

Manufactured in the United States of America
1-50690-50109-3/29/2022